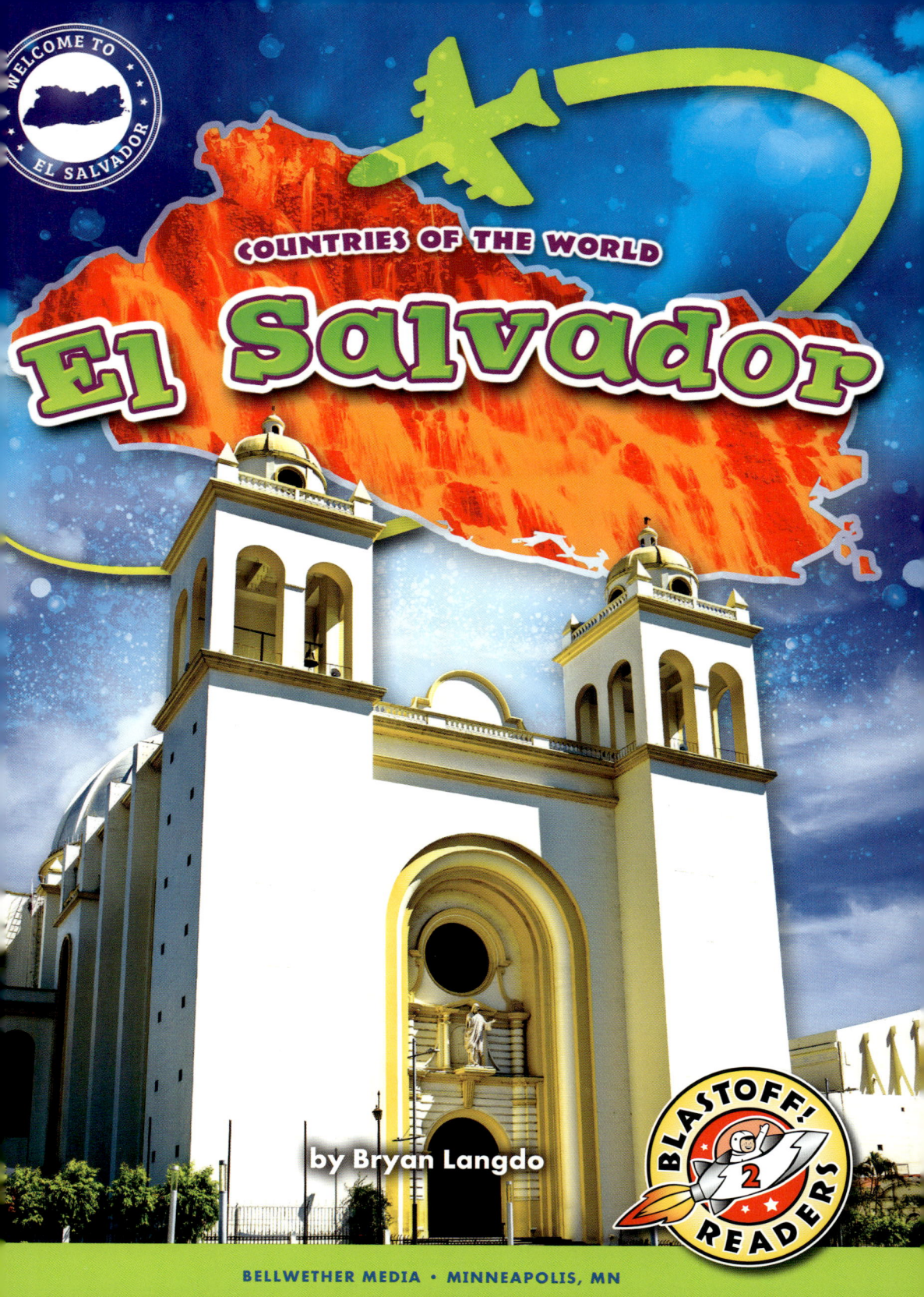

WELCOME TO EL SALVADOR

COUNTRIES OF THE WORLD

El Salvador

by Bryan Langdo

BLASTOFF! READERS 2

BELLWETHER MEDIA • MINNEAPOLIS, MN

Blastoff! Readers are carefully developed by literacy experts to build reading stamina and move students toward fluency by combining standards-based content with developmentally appropriate text.

LEVELS

Level 1 provides the most support through repetition of high-frequency words, light text, predictable sentence patterns, and strong visual support.

Level 2 offers early readers a bit more challenge through varied sentences, increased text load, and text-supportive special features.

Level 3 advances early-fluent readers toward fluency through increased text load, less reliance on photos, advancing concepts, longer sentences, and more complex special features.

★ **Blastoff! Universe**

Reading Level

Grade K → Grades 1–3 → Grade 4

This edition first published in 2025 by Bellwether Media, Inc.

No part of this publication may be reproduced in whole or in part without written permission of the publisher. For information regarding permission, write to Bellwether Media, Inc., Attention: Permissions Department, 6012 Blue Circle Drive, Minnetonka, MN 55343.

Library of Congress Cataloging-in-Publication Data

Names: Langdo, Bryan, author.
Title: El Salvador / by Bryan Langdo.
Description: Minneapolis, MN : Bellwether Media, [2025] | Series: Blastoff! Readers: Countries of the World | Includes bibliographical references and index. | Audience: Ages 5-8 | Audience: Grades 2-3 | Summary: "Relevant images match informative text in this introduction to El Salvador. Intended for students in kindergarten through third grade"– Provided by publisher.
Identifiers: LCCN 2024012089 (print) | LCCN 2024012090 (ebook) | ISBN 9798886879834 (library binding) | ISBN 9781644879153 (ebook)
Subjects: LCSH: El Salvador–Juvenile literature.
Classification: LCC F1483.2 .L36 2025 (print) | LCC F1483.2 (ebook) | DDC 972.84–dc23/eng/20240319
LC record available at https://lccn.loc.gov/2024012089
LC ebook record available at https://lccn.loc.gov/2024012090

Text copyright © 2025 by Bellwether Media, Inc. BLASTOFF! READERS and associated logos are trademarks and/or registered trademarks of Bellwether Media, Inc. Bellwether Media is a division of Chrysalis Education Group.

Editor: Suzane Nguyen   Designer: Laura Sowers

Printed in the United States of America, North Mankato, MN.

Table of Contents

All About El Salvador	4
Land and Animals	6
Life in El Salvador	12
El Salvador Facts	20
Glossary	22
To Learn More	23
Index	24

All About El Salvador

San Salvador

El Salvador is the smallest country in Central America. Its capital is San Salvador.

The country is often known as the Land of **Volcanoes**!

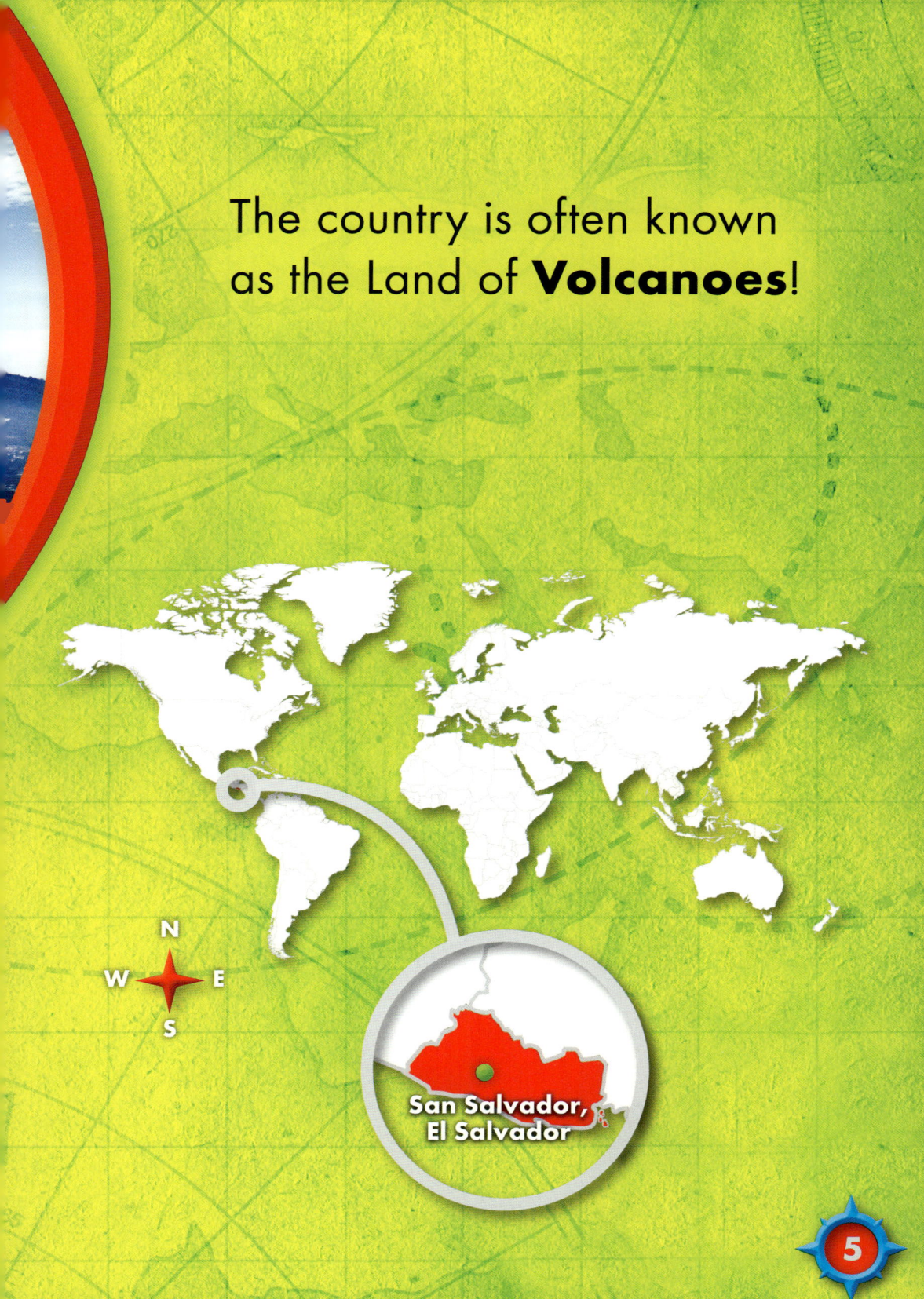

San Salvador, El Salvador

Land and Animals

Mountains cover most of El Salvador. The highest volcano is Santa Ana Volcano.

A **cloud forest** sits in the northwest. The south has a coastal **plain**.

coastal plain

Santa Ana Volcano

Height: 7,812 feet (2,381 meters) tall
Famous For: being the highest volcano in El Salvador and a popular place to hike

El Salvador is a **tropical** country. It is warm all year. But the air is cooler in the mountains.

Heavy rains fall during the wet season.

Many animals live in El Salvador's forests. Spider monkeys swing from trees.

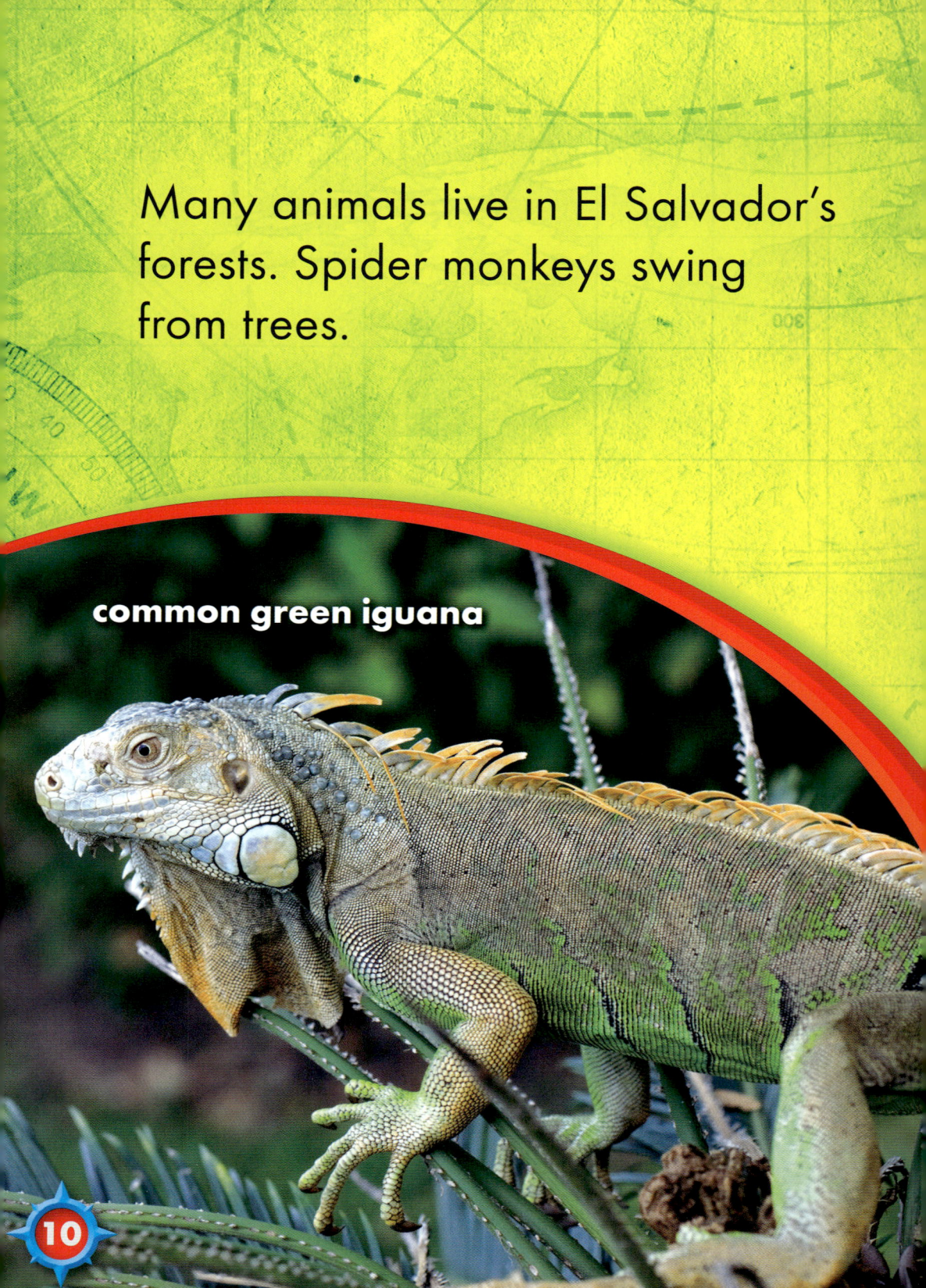

common green iguana

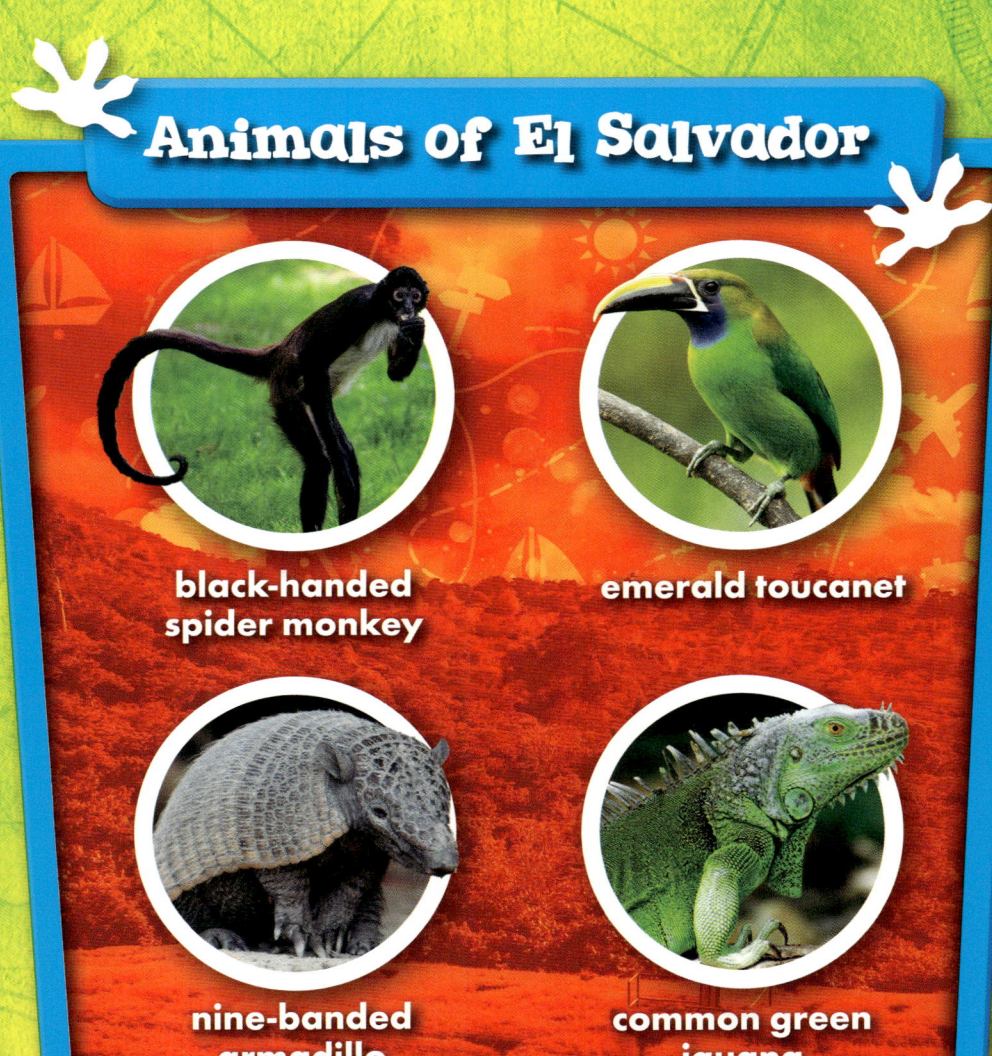

Animals of El Salvador

black-handed spider monkey

emerald toucanet

nine-banded armadillo

common green iguana

Toucans snack on fruit. Armadillos roam **grasslands**. Iguanas lie in the sun.

Life in El Salvador

Most Salvadorans are Spanish and **Indigenous**. Spanish is the main language.

Many Salvadorans live in cities. About half the people are **Roman Catholic**.

Roman Catholic church

Salvadorans enjoy the arts. They play **traditional** music. They make pottery.

Salvadorans love soccer. Basketball and boxing are popular, too.

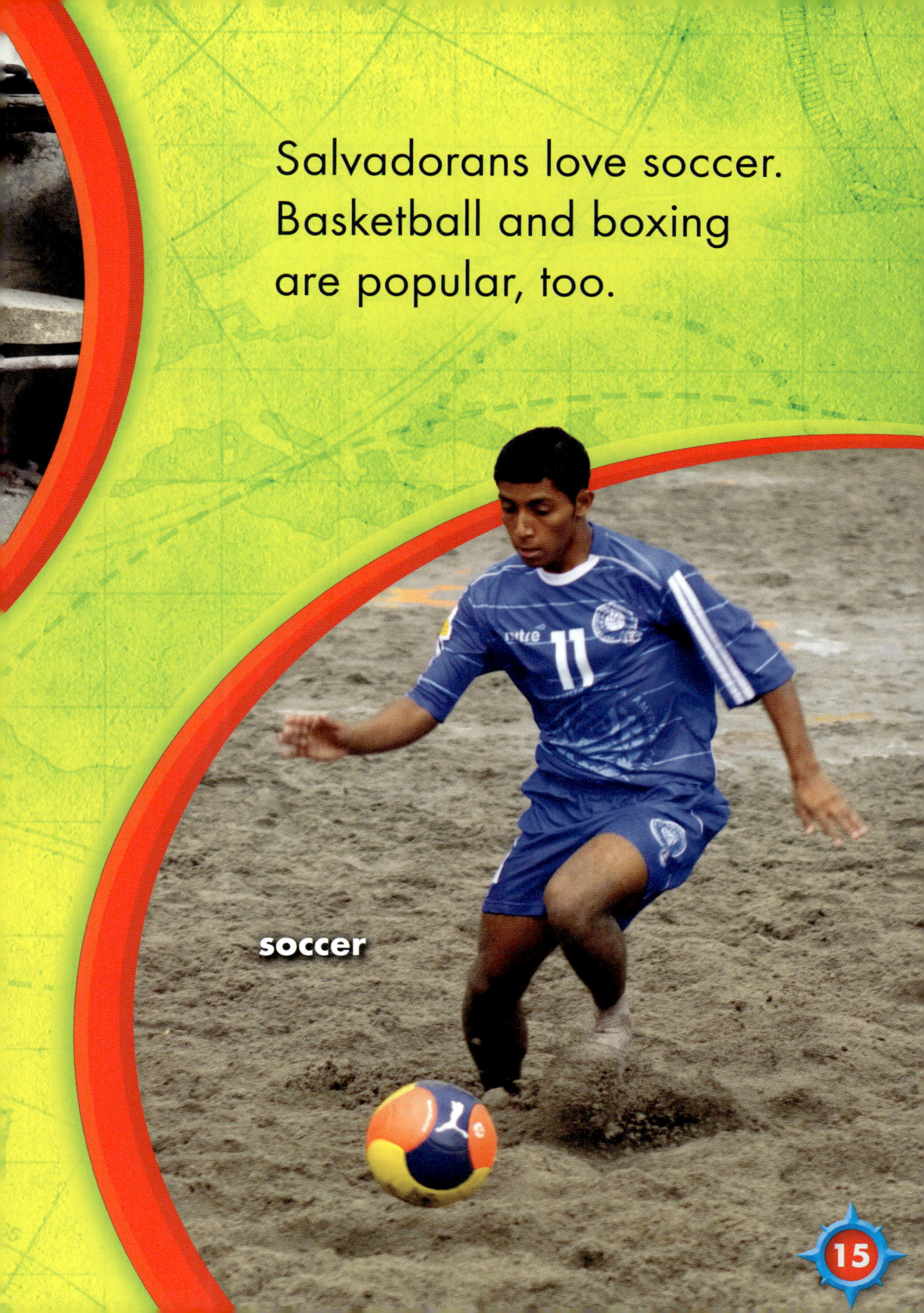

soccer

Many Salvadoran dishes include *frijoles*, or beans. *Casamiento* is a rice and beans dish.

Salvadoran Foods

frijoles

casamiento

pupusas

sopa de pata

pupusas

Pupusas are stuffed tortillas. *Sopa de pata* is a soup. It is made with cow's feet!

Independence Day

August 6 is Fiesta de San Salvador. A parade carries a statue of Jesus Christ.

September 15 is Independence Day. Marching bands perform. Salvadorans love their country!

El Salvador Facts

Size:
8,124 square miles
(21,041 square kilometers)

Population:
6,602,370 (2023)

National Holiday:
Independence Day (September 15)

Main Language:
Spanish

Capital City:
San Salvador

Famous Face

Name: Ana Villafañe

Famous For: singer and actress who has performed on Broadway

Religions

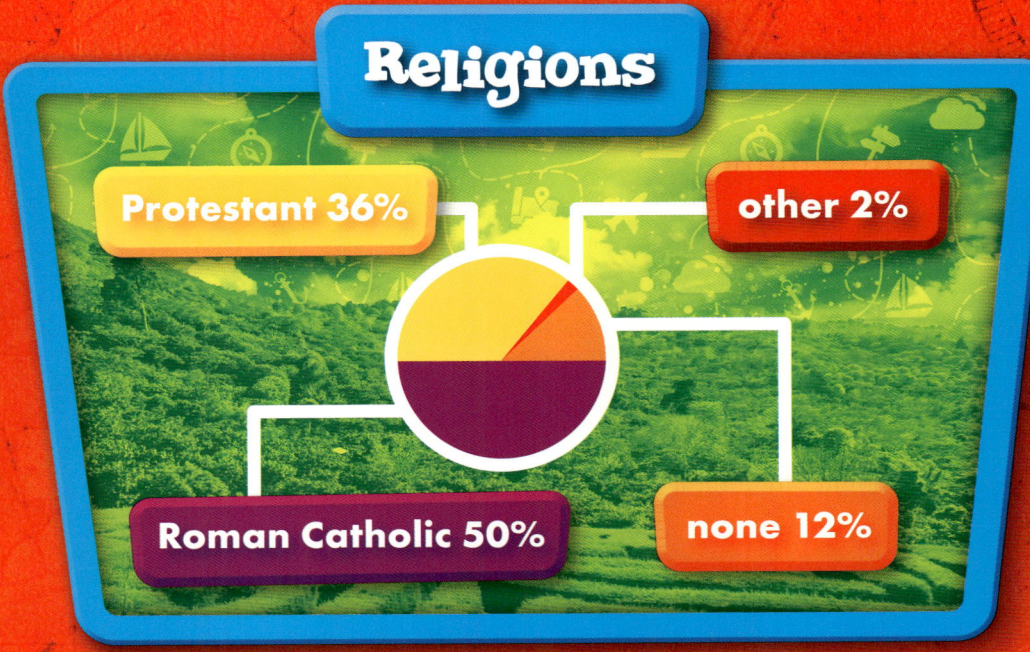

- Protestant 36%
- other 2%
- Roman Catholic 50%
- none 12%

Top Landmarks

Monument to the Divine Savior of the World

Plaza Libertad

Tazumal Archaeological Park

Glossary

cloud forest—a mountain forest that is wet and cloudy

grasslands—lands covered with grasses and other soft plants with few bushes or trees

Indigenous—related to people originally from an area

plain—an area of flat land with few trees

Roman Catholic—people belonging or relating to the Christian church that is led by the pope

traditional—related to customs, ideas, or beliefs handed down from one generation to the next

tropical—having to do with a place that is hot and wet

volcanoes—holes in the earth; when a volcano erupts, hot ash, gas, or melted rock called lava shoots out.

To Learn More

AT THE LIBRARY

Fowler, Leona. *Toucans and Other Birds*. Buffalo, N.Y.: Enslow Publishing, 2024.

Gibbons, Gail. *Volcanoes*. New York, N.Y.: Holiday House, 2021.

Klepeis, Alicia Z. *El Salvador*. New York, N.Y.: Cavendish Square Publishing, 2020.

ON THE WEB

Factsurfer.com gives you a safe, fun way to find more information.

1. Go to www.factsurfer.com.

2. Enter "El Salvador" into the search box and click 🔍.

3. Select your book cover to see a list of related content.

Index

animals, 10, 11
arts, 14
basketball, 15
boxing, 15
capital (see San Salvador)
Central America, 4
cities, 12
cloud forest, 6
coastal plain, 6
El Salvador facts, 20–21
Fiesta de San Salvador, 18
food, 16, 17
forests, 10
grasslands, 11
Independence Day, 18, 19
map, 5
mountains, 6, 8

music, 14
people, 12, 14, 15
pottery, 14
rains, 9
Roman Catholic, 12
San Salvador, 4, 5
Santa Ana Volcano, 6, 7
say hello, 13
soccer, 15
Spanish, 12, 13
volcanoes, 5, 6, 7

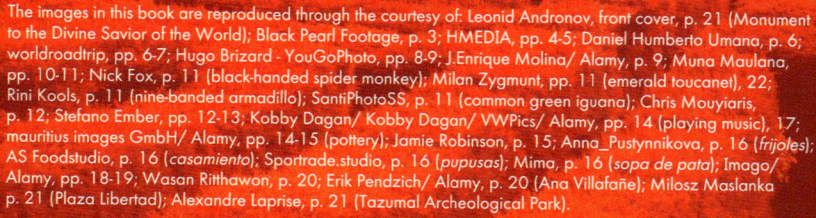

The images in this book are reproduced through the courtesy of: Leonid Andronov, front cover, p. 21 (Monument to the Divine Savior of the World); Black Pearl Footage, p. 3; HMEDIA, pp. 4-5; Daniel Humberto Umana, p. 6; worldroadtrip, pp. 6-7; Hugo Brizard - YouGoPhoto, pp. 8-9; J.Enrique Molina/ Alamy, p. 9; Muna Maulana, pp. 10-11; Nick Fox, p. 11 (black-handed spider monkey); Milan Zygmunt, pp. 11 (emerald toucanet), 22; Rini Kools, p. 11 (nine-banded armadillo); SantiPhotoSS, p. 11 (common green iguana); Chris Mouyiaris, p. 12; Stefano Ember, pp. 12-13; Kobby Dagan/ Kobby Dagan/ VWPics/ Alamy, pp. 14 (playing music), 17; mauritius images GmbH/ Alamy, pp. 14-15 (pottery); Jamie Robinson, p. 15; Anna_Pustynnikova, p. 16 (*frijoles*); AS Foodstudio, p. 16 (*casamiento*); Sportrade.studio, p. 16 (*pupusas*); Mima, p. 16 (*sopa de pata*); Imago/ Alamy, pp. 18-19; Wasan Ritthawon, p. 20; Erik Pendzich/ Alamy, p. 20 (Ana Villafañe); Milosz Maslanka p. 21 (Plaza Libertad); Alexandre Laprise, p. 21 (Tazumal Archeological Park).